Dylan Watts
Gerhard Dollansky

Forget About Selling

Dylan Watts
Gerhard Dollansky

Forget About Selling

Watts, Dylan:
Forget About Selling / Dylan Watts ; Gerhard Dollansky
Publisher: Georgi-Verlag, Taufkirchen, Germany : 2016
ISBN 978-1537031439

Edition History:
1st German ed. March 2002 Title: Vergiss das Verkaufen
2nd German rev. ed. March 2016: Vergiss das Verkaufen
English ed. August 2016: Forget About Selling
This English edition is based upon the German original, but was completely revised and extended for the English speaking reader.
www.forget-about-selling.com

© 2016 Dr. Gerhard Dollansky,
Im Mitterfeld 23, 82024 Taufkirchen, Germany
All rights reserved

Cover design:	© 2016 Jens Wehde
Photo page 81:	© 2015 Jens Wehde, www.wehde.de
Photo page 83:	© 2015 Birgit Kritzer, Fotostudio KS 36, www.people-fotos.de

Printed by CreateSpace

ISBN 978-1537031439

Content

Foreword 7
Introduction 9
Create Attraction 12
Make Selling a Game 15
Take Small Steps 18
Get Your Way by Giving In 21
Educate People 24
Entertain your Clients 27
Give Unique Gifts 30
Make People Right 32
Share your Passion 36
Learn the Art of Dialogue 38
Surprise your Clients 40
Make your Clients' Goals your Own 43
Build a Team 46
Give Acknowledgements 49
Remember Why You Sell 52
Be a Coach and Trainer 55
Learn How to Recognize Vitality 58
Build your Business Network 61
Tell Stories that Create Curiosity 65
Be Flexible in Changing Times 69
Train Like an Athlete 72
Make Sales your Priority 75
Expand your Horizons 78
About the Authors 81

Many thanks to all the people who participated in Forget About Selling seminars during the past 15 years, who accompany us on our way of People Growing, provide feedback and helped to improve this material.

Thanks to the Sage University team, to Sandra Jantzen, Klana Andreas Ludwig, Jens Wehde, Flavia Zaka, Jessica Bailey Sanchez and Glo Villarreal for all your great support and insights.

Special thanks to our coach and mentor. We gratefully acknowledge your belief in us as a significant influence in our life and work.

Love and gratitude to our children Markus, Michele, Jacqueline, Alexander, Henrik and Luis.

Foreword

Trust is the most essential skill in relationship selling. Dylan Watts and Gerhard Dollansky rank among the most honorable men I have ever had the privilege to know. Their approach to winning customer loyalty is based on their own high standards of professional conduct in business and in every arena of life.

This brief book is a glimpse of a future in which traditional selling techniques are becoming as obsolete as the typewriter. The first time you read it you will naturally absorb the information that conforms with the way you view buying and selling. If you revisit these pages occasionally over several months you will begin to notice innovative themes that emerge like the hidden 3-d images in a Magic Eye poster. Before you realize it your eyes will soften to reveal unexpected structures in the tones and vibrations that people exchange as they negotiate more effective ways to communicate.

Good salesmanship makes a sale. Great salesmanship wins the kind of trust that pervades emerging business systems and lasts for an entire career. I hope you enjoy this brief book and that you are fortunate enough to collaborate with the authors.

M. Sage

Introduction

In the current service-centered age, selling is more important than ever. As the expectations of clients rise, the selling process itself is altered. Do you know today's rules of selling? A first hint: product-knowledge and selling-techniques are not enough.

Nearly all books on selling focus solely on selling-techniques. This book, however, specializes on the manner of dealing with people. Sales-training teaches typical techniques, for example in the realm of winning over clients or closing a deal. These brief chapters take you to the next level by focusing on the quality of relationships between people.

Salespeople are often content to learn techniques because these are comfortable and easy to use. However, few people enjoy when sales techniques are applied on them. It feels false, when a salesperson resorts to an old deal-closing technique. Superficial tactics strip people of their dignity. No one wants to feel manipulated by those who are just "doing their thing".

Clients today are drawn toward advisors and coaches that support their desires and wishes. They are repelled by sellers who push too hard.

Selling is the most important skill you can learn in order to succeed in business. Learn as many techniques as possible, but keep this in mind: the ability to establish life-long trust with people who will want to do business with you for years to come is the epitome of selling in this service-centered age. The moment trust is established, you will sell, even when your competition offers something different or better. Staying true to your word is better than saying the right thing.

Products and services are being constantly improved. Regardless of how strongly you believe in your product, there are always plenty of alternatives. The modern market is overflowing with other products and services that already have the trust of their customers. The only possible variation is you.

The business tempo is running at an ever-faster pace. Deep knowledge of people grants you a much needed advantage. You will be astonished how, through the use of these innovative tips, you can gain the trust of your customers by applying these innovative tips. We feel privileged to present to you the next level in the evolution of business relations.

In less than one month, you can achieve better results and experience more professional fulfillment by reading one of these innovative tips daily. By applying the tools offered in the following pages to your work, you will gain a new perspective on what works in professional sales and what does not.

This book is designed to awaken you rather than provide all the answers. Each client is unique and by asking the right questions, you will bring deep and empathetic abilities to your sales process.

Across industries, we have learned much from our clients. Whether a sole-proprietor of a Turkish vegetable shop, a mid-size car-dealership or a thriving software company, all businesses have a common thread: they deal with people who want to be respected, valued and acknowledged.

Progress in technology has determined every turning point in history. Large battles have always been won with ever-better technology. Systems of superior quality have overhauled old ones. No one armed with merely a sword would be taken seriously in a modern battlefield. Until now, salespeople show up to work with techniques developed in the 1950s.

In *Forget about Selling*, we present a powerful new way of systemic thinking: Systems theory encompasses the complexity of organizations. Those who understand the greater context of events, will easily outperform those who are focused on mere survival. This book shows you a proven path to build long-lasting professional friendships through building a network.

The one-time sell is an illusion. The most successful people become an endless resource to their clients. Some people have a special way of bonding with others. If they can learn it, so can you.

Superior social capacities are at the heart of building professional relationships. By blending coaching skills into the selling process, you will inspire other people by winning their trust.

Create Attraction

Curiosity moves people. If people feel that they are being manipulated, they go into a state of resistance. When you awaken their curiosity, they will eagerly purchase your product.

Tom Sawyer created the right attitude to paint the fence with enthusiasm. Through his charm he let everyone know how much he loved doing work that is ordinarily considered unpleasant. Whistling and laughing, he attracted the attention of his friends. Seemingly reluctantly, he allowed them to participate in his task but only after they had paid for this privilege

People are curious by nature. Simply by paying attention to others you activate their curiosity. What is your job?" or "What are you doing for a living?" Most people are eager to tell you their story. Listen carefully when they tell you what they are doing with their time. Wait. And after a short break almost every person will echo. "What about you? What are you doing?"

The closer attention you pay, the more intensive their reaction. Words are important. But the real attraction is your deep interest in another person. Create attraction by increasing your attention.

Curiosity is the strongest force of evolution. Every species and system that reached the next level of evolution did it by being curious enough to adapt.

The first step in the new art of selling is to create curiosity about you and your product or service. Your honest interest in a person is a sure way to awaken their curiosity.

The old way of selling is based on manipulation. The new art of selling uses the element of surprise to catch the attention of the client.

If you step into a room and express what you do for a living, hardly anyone will react. Only these people who are interested in what you are doing will give you their attention. Automatically you invited the curious people to come closer. By creating curiosity you find the people who truly appreciate you and your work.

The best way to become an attractive person is to find a mentor who helps people create a better life. If you are lucky to meet an effective salesperson with this talent, find a way to spend time with that individual.

You increase the power of a magnet by bringing it into the field of a stronger one.

When I was 35 years old, I had the good fortune to meet a man who later became my mentor. I was fascinated by the sincere interest he showed in me—talking with him made me feel as though time stopped and that I stood at the center of the universe. The curious conversations we had, left me with a deep sense of appreciation that was a much needed balm for my soul. I knew immediately that I wanted to learn to speak with people with an equally sincere and earnest interest. My mentor showed me a multi-layered process called "the interview". By posing a series of questions, you can reveal what the interviewee truly desires. My desire to learn this process was so strong that I have spent countless days over the past 15 years working with him.

Make Selling a Game

Most people take selling too seriously. Many are afraid of rejection. This unconscious attitude burdens the relationship with your customer.

When you turn selling into a game, you bring an exciting accent of lightness in this exchange. Use this pleasure principle and a completely new circle of clients will show up.

The finest games are pure fun. A well-prepared game draws the attention to shared pleasure. When you are playing, your laughter is natural. You relax completely. People hear the vitality in your voice. A true sense of play awakens your child-like lightness. It softens your face and makes you glow.

You can develop the discipline to change work into play. Most of us tend to be excessively serious and to turn events into problems. Goals can quickly turn into stressful worries. Play introduces the element of balance in sales. You can learn to work just for fun and to be paid for playing.

There are different kinds of games. Some are more effective than others. Zero-sum games have no winners. Seller and buyer both lose. Each tries to acquire more from the other and both feel cheated. Lose-Lose strategies are usually fruitless. Lose-win strategies are somewhat better. The salesperson overcomes objections and wins in the short term. But in the long term the reputation of the product suffers. And be sure: If someone loses, the reputation of every salesperson suffers.

The best games are based on a win-win philosophy. You win by helping others win. In these games, strategy is more important than tactics. We spend a lot of time creating situations in which our clients win together with us. This time is a good investment because we are able to offer our service with little or no resistance.

In school we learned to defeat others, to get better grades or higher scores. Competition is important for our development, but a top-seller goes beyond the dog-eat-dog approach by building systems of collaboration in which everyone wins.

It requires special wisdom to win continuously by helping others win. Study the strategies of top-sellers who easily generate referrals. Write down a list of the best salespeople you know and employ them as coaches. Study their rhythms and tones. Greater sensitivity will give you a path to go deeper until you see the whole field of information from which they make their decisions.

Deep learning can take months to learn and years to perfect. But the return on your time investment will lift you to the top of your profession. You will be surprised how profitable it is when you develop a profound understanding of yourself and others.

Hakan, a Turkish wholesaler, rejected an offer because my price was too high.
"It is an excellent product!" I claimed.
"That's what I am expecting anyway" said the client. I thought about how I could convince him to purchase from me.
"If you buy the product and accept my price, then I will kiss your feet at our next meeting." Hakan laughed.
"That is not necessary. I simply want a lower price!"
I turned to my last tactic. "I can sadly not change my price. It is firmly set. But especially for you I will do the following: I will now step out of the office, enter the hall and personally hand-sign your palette of vegetables. When you show up to work tomorrow, this hand-signed palette with your very own vegetables will be waiting for you."
Hakan laughed again and said: "Only you could come up with such a wild idea!" He took a small break and finally said "Okay fine. Send me the palette! And believe me, I will try this out with my customers as well!"

Take Small Steps

Instead of pushing yourself to get results in your business, calm down. Start learning how to build a web of trustful people.

Growing a business is like growing kids. You do it with patience, love and devotion. Very few people get rich quick, despite the many who aspire to easy money. This is a big mistake. Think whether you would feed your kids more food than they need to make them grow faster than the other kids.

Your business network is a family system. Every business has its own growing pattern. Fulfillment comes from enjoying each stage along the way. Don't hurry through your life.

When you fall into *quantity* thinking you are only busy and your timer looks full. Busy-ness is not business. But when you bring *quality* awareness to the game, your business partners, associates, and customers will bring great pleasure into your career Relationships that are built quickly will also end fast. When you grow them slowly you develop strong roots. Relationships you cultivate carefully, will live long. Results occur as a side effect of great professional friendships.

It hurts a lot if you have to fight for every single deal. According to the traditional point of view, every transaction is a battle. You conduct business as a war of attrition. Pressure shows up everywhere in your life.

In the new service economy selling is more comparable with farming. First you plough the soil, plant the seed, and cultivate the crop. When the season changes, there comes a time for the harvest. Authentic results occur in their own time, but over the span of your career they endure longer and deliver prosperity that lasts a lifetime.

Some people are worth growing, and others cause more harm than good. Don`t be afraid to pull out the weeds in your field. Say goodbye to the clients who bring you down and talk badly about you. Maybe you have to let go of some profit right now if you leave destructive people behind. Be kind and always show respect when you part ways with a friend. But your honesty and forthrightness will clear the way for a healthy and strong field for the future.

Because the new art of selling is complex, you need more time to learn people skills. Observe how babies learn. They experience through moving their fingers and toes as they reach for things they want to grasp. One skill builds on the other until the child can move effortlessly.

There is an organic sequence in this learning process. Crawling comes before walking. Through continuous improvement you build a fertile field for a successful career.

If you increase your sales only by 1% per week you will raise your turnover at 50 % per year.

Take the time to provide outstanding service to your best clients. Be known for your reliability. Remember, trust is the source of power in business.

Stay fresh and relaxed and don`t overburden yourself. Your degree of relaxation will influence the people you need. Learn from the story of the rabbit and the turtle. The race is not always won by the fastest.

As a small farmer I had a clear vision: I wanted to become rich. I began in the summer of 1988 by selling cabbage in the streets of Cologne. Each day, I drove with my small trailer to the nearby city. One of the customers told me about the wholesale markets in the city. It did not take long before I transitioned from serving the end-customer to serving the Turkish wholesale merchants in hypermarkets. Because of my conscientious service, my clients recommended me to their friends and colleagues across Germany. Three years later I had a network of 30 clients in hypermarkets country-wide.

Step by step, we worked on the improvement of the product and service. Fourteen years later we celebrated our innovation's visible success. The fulfillment that came from my friendships was also accompanied by financial freedom. My premium-product, the Jaroma-Cabbage, found its entry into supermarket throughout Europe.

Get Your Way by Giving In

The most powerful force in sales is yielding. Wise women have always known that the partner who is led in dancing decides the directions and pace of the dance. The same principle applies in sales, where people lead by making choices in response to a receptive seller. You can improve your sales tremendously by discerning when you should lead overtly and when you should lead by yielding.

Imagine a table around which sit 7 bosses. Six of them hold strong opinions, which they defend stubbornly. One has learned to yield and to be receptive to other perspectives.

Every opinionated person will prefer to have the yielding person on his side. There is a time for power through force. But greater success comes to those who can be soft at the right time.

Try this experiment. Stand back-to-back with a partner and push against each other. Each one tries to dominate and control the other person by intensity and nimble maneuvering. After a short testing of power you can begin to yield. Allow yourself to be pushed until you are close to the wall. As you turn to avoid the obstacle, your partner will follow you. In this moment your body will feel how yielding works. The one who is yielding selects the direction of the interaction.

Everyone wants to be heard. If you listen carefully you will earn the trust of important people. Selling doesn't mean to push your product down somebody´s throat. The new art of selling is an invitation for strong people to become part of your business network.

Protect your business network like your family. Without any doubt you can follow this sentence in business as in life. Your clients are not your enemies. They are responsible friends who need protection and guidance.

Top sellers have a large bag of tools and techniques. If you are able to yield, you have a tool others don´t know how to use.

Selling means to find out what clients need and to help them get it. When we follow our client´s desires we become a worthy part of their life.

Anybody can push other people. They might get their way temporarily. But they will scorch their territory. The best salespeople have the sensitivity to assist people to go their way. Speak clearly. If someone pressures you, hold your stance. When you reach an impasse, then slowly begin to give in to get your way. And then steer, in a measured manner, to reach your goal.

Compare a car that is only able to drive forward with a car that is also able to drive in reverse. Yielding doubles your possibilities and quadruples your advantage in selling.

Once a customer called me complaining that the last delivery contained too many small cabbage-heads. Some were rotten. I told him: "I believe you."
"No, you don't believe me, come over and take a look for yourself!"
I repeated: "I believe you."
"I will call over my brother. He will attest to it."
"Okay, you don't have to call your brother. If you say it was a bad batch, then that must be true. If the cabbage was not good, you know, I take responsibility for it."
After this he admitted that there were only a few bad heads.
"Count how many. I would like to pay you for these."
"You don't need to. It's not even worth discussing."

Educate People

People love seminars that deliver valuable information. Take every chance to teach a group in a general area or to introduce them to a special product or service.

While people generally mistrust salespeople instinctively, they trust teachers. When you teach people you automatically earn their trust by offering them valuable information for free.

The new service-economy is based on personal experiences. People want to attend events that change their lives. The best way to educate is through entertainment. People learn by having fun. Tupperware started a revolution by doing home-parties to sell their products. Now, computer companies and car showrooms find new clients and renew the trust of their regulars by offering them entertaining and informative events, such as car-rallies, trainings and seminars.

Education can take different forms. Coaching is the process of transforming work into play. The coaching field is changing continuously. People hire personal trainers and professional coaches who help to make the right decisions and hold them accountable for results. As a professional salesperson you are in the best position to offer coaching.

Be a partner to your clients when they are setting a new course. Coach them in your specific field as a free service. You don´t need an academic degree. Your experiences are unique on earth. We can learn as much from workers as from professors. You can share your knowledge about computers, music, nature, or other themes. Share your knowledge of everything that you are interested in.

Often we teach what we want to learn. The best way to become better at selling is to offer sales trainings to people who are new in sales. Thereby you have countless possibilities to repeat and rehearse the basic skills.

Education is derived from the Latin word "e-duco" which means to bring something out to the surface—something that is already there. If you are interested in what people know and what they want to learn, you will earn their trust and lifelong friendship.

It was a Wednesday evening, and my first seminar project stood before me. A two-hour presentation was planned. I recall quite clearly these beginnings of my career as a trainer. Up until this point I had sold vegetables to vegetable-vendors. Now everything was about to change. I was learning how to grow people.

At that first sales training I was very nervous. It was unfamiliar to stand in front of people and be judged by them. It was not my vegetables that took center stage this time, it was myself.

The evening unfolded under the theme: Forget About Selling! *How can I read people? How can I move people? How can I deepen relationships between them?*

This was my first seminar evening. And as this night came to an end, my self-perception changed. That experience altered my personality, and transformed the effect that I had on others. I was no longer a salesperson and businessman. All of a sudden, I was also a coach and a trainer. When Forget About Selling *came out in print, I was also an author. I had stepped into completely new territory.*

Instantly my customers saw me in a very new light. I was invited to take part in important decisions. They would say: "On this matter we should ask Dylan, he has written about this; he has held presentations on this matter; he has the theory; he has learned this." People referred to me as though I knew more and had more to offer than before.

Being able to fit into this new role and teach people new things, to share my experiences with them—this was very enriching for me.

Entertain your Clients

Education and entertainment go hand in hand. The best education is entertaining and the best entertainment is educational.

People are born to experience pleasure; they are attracted to entertainment. We love the people who make us laugh. Friends entertain and like each other. They make plans for common events. They share something that is much more than business. With the right sense of humor, you can share your valuable product or information in a fresh way. Fun generates attention.

Every child is a natural born entertainer. Children do not work. They don't practice. They simply play. This playfulness is contagious to everyone around them. By playing with your clients (your friends), you help them get what they want and what you want at the same time you entertain each other.

In the past, film stars and sports idols became heroes. Today, the heroes are business people who become famous. Steve Jobs, Hasso Plattner, Mark Zuckerberg, Richard Branson and Elon Musk are all famous personalities. Their performances inspire us. We love to speak and to read about them.

There are no natural born entertainers. Famous people developed the skill to entertain people. A true entertainer doesn´t grasp for the attention of other people; they focus their attention on the people themselves. That generosity makes them attractive. To focus your attention on your client is key in successful selling.

Commercials are sold through entertainment. The big TV channels know that pleasure and sales support each other. The pleasure in socializing is a good combination for the advertising of your product or service.

Don´t pretend something. Just be happy. Learn to enjoy other people. You are a friendly warmhearted person. Let everyone know this.

Some years ago a client asked me to accompany him at a company delegation from China. So I accompanied him to his meeting with the seven Chinese guests. As expected, the conversation also involved non-business related things. I told them a humorous story of an old woman, who placed a million dollar bet against Rockefeller. The bet was that within a week, Rockefeller's testicles would become rectangular. Rockefeller saw this as easily won money, and agreed to the bet. After a week, the lady appeared with a Chinese man to Rockefeller's office to decide on the results of the bet. Before she had to resign to having lost the bet, she insisted on having proof of it. Pressured, Rockefeller had to drop his pants and present the evidence. Naturally the woman had lost the bet. The man that accompanied her, that until this moment had said nothing, suddenly swooned. At Rockefeller's plea to explain what was happening, the woman said: "I placed a three million dollar bet with Mr. Wang that on Tuesday I would have Rockefeller by the balls."

A short time ago, I wrote to one of the men from this delegation to support me in organizing a training session and presentation in Shanghai. In his e-mail response, he said: "Of course, you shared that funny joke about the old woman and the Chinese player. I remember you very well!"

Give Unique Gifts

Words are the two dimensional portrait of our feelings. Gifts, however, are the three-dimensional sculptures that represent our feelings. Gift giving shows that you care about someone else. A gift delivers appreciation. People see that you took the time to think of them. Your choice of size, color and form leaves an impression.

Gifts are small symbols. They have their own message. Endearing objects speak for themselves. People are touched by them. A good choice for a gift shows that you invested some time and attention to your connection.

The best gift is not a card with the logo of your company. The best gift is a unique and inexpensive gesture that shows real feelings and a deep interest in another person.

Humans interact in two different economic systems. One is the money for product economy. We spend money and get products or services in exchange. The other is the gift economy. This practice is one we usually only share with our family or close friends. By combining both the product and gift economy with our clients, they feel appreciated.

Friedrich, one of my best clients, faced a significant challenge with his enterprise. He was at risk of losing his business. The situation demanded a form of leadership and a forceful way of conducting business that he wasn't familiar with. I bought a paperback book that I handed over to him in our next meeting. It was the story of Ernest Shackleton, who in 1915 during a South Pole expedition was faced with a shipwreck that presented a seemingly hopeless situation for him and his men. The book described how Shackleton led 27 men, who were trapped in Antarctica over a period of two years. He brought them back to safety without losing a single person.

Friedrich's firm overcame the peak of the crisis after eight months. By working together they saw light at the end of the tunnel. In one of our meetings Friedrich said to me with teary eyes: "Thank you Dylan for giving me this book! During this entire period I had Shackleton in mind, and I thought, if he could manage to get out of a crisis, then I damn well can too!"

Make People Right

Every person has an opinion. Behind their opinions you will find kind and warmhearted people. Our opinions separate us from one another, just as they separate you and me.

People are attached to their opinions. The fact is that most of them believe that their opinion has something to do with reality. If you contradict their opinion, you will have the opportunity to share your opinion. By trying to be right, you will lose their connection.

You can be right or you can be rich. Both together is not possible. You can fight for your political and religious principles, but it will cost you the trust and connection of your clients. I am always delighted when someone tells me his opinion. "Interesting!" I answer, or "I never considered this aspect before."

I have my own points of view, but there is no space for them in the selling process.

It is helpful to like people. Whether you are well-informed or badly informed, educated or not, I am fascinated by you. Your point of view makes you unique.

In my mind I am amazed how many people hold opposing ideas. Imagine how boring the world would be if everyone thought like you or me. I love the variety the world has to offer. I try never to agree with someone. And I try my best not to criticize, to blame, or to give advice.

Your opinion gives me a new point of view from which to see life. It is part of you, like your arms and legs. To appreciate other points of view opens up a new level of communication. In the moment I buy your opinion, you are open to buy my product.

Top sellers maintain a cool mind and a warm heart. They realize the value of your way of looking at things. There is nothing more fascinating than listening to someone who is telling you his idea of life. If you can read the secret code of another person, you can sense an invitation to friendship and business. Top-sellers are looking for a sign that can help their clients embrace a larger perspective.

Every word shows the direction to sell people what they really want. To agree with everyone and everything makes you appear weak. To accept everyone makes you professional.

By truly listening and saying: "I see it in a different way," I can have a difference of opinion by not being unpleasant.

I don´t allow myself to think or say someone is wrong. I know that the person is somehow right, even if I cannot see it right away.

The sales representative spoke every day with her wholesale customers. One customer in Stuttgart received two tons of cucumbers daily. Suddenly, they stopped purchasing. My colleague called and received this response: "We have enough cucumbers." It was obviously a flimsy response, not allowing my colleague to get to the reasons for this disconnect. If they had enough cucumbers, then they were delivered by somebody else. My colleague left the matter alone. After a few days, I called the customer.

"What is the matter?" I asked.
> *"Everything is fine. It's all good."*

"So, what is the matter then?"
> *"Nothing, we are happy. Business is quiet.*
> *We don't need anything at the moment.*
> *Call again next week."*

"I'd like to know immediately what is wrong. Have you been offended?"
> *"Yes, in fact, a little."*

"Thank you. What has happened then?"
> *"Last week the cucumbers weren't good."*

"Why didn't you say anything about it?"
> *"I told the woman in your office."*

"And what did she say?"
> *"She said: This cannot be.*
> *We only sell good cucumbers."*

My colleague did not hear the complaint. The customer could not accept this, and by refusing to purchase cucumbers from us, they showed us who ultimately had control. Had I not been attentive, I would have lost a customer who purchased two tons daily.

The moment in which I am cross with someone, my mood has consequences. I pay the price for it. In sales, the effect of not taking signs seriously, can easily be measured by the numbers. If someone is overlooked, this will cost money. When I am alert, I can respond quickly. The capacity to fix the situation is always in your hands.

"We are sorry that we did not believe you. What can I do so that you continue to buy cucumbers from us?"
"You don't have to do anything, it's fine.
I still have cucumbers today.
We'll call you tomorrow to place an order."

Acknowledging and not contradicting is key. Acknowledge and solve the customer's problem. Denial damages the mutual trust. The excuse that no one else complained is not a satisfying explanation for any customer.

Share your Passion

Selling is easy when you sell to people with whom you share the same values. All people have the same desire for a better world. Deep down every person has the desire for peace and prosperity. People choose different ways to serve mankind.

If you know your values, you have a sound basis for your passion. You will work together best with the people who have similar values. When people feel that the purpose of your work is far beyond earning money, they will show you profound humanity.

Do you want to protect nature? Is your family important for you? Don´t exaggerate, but let people know what is in your heart.

It doesn't work to feign interest in something simply to earn money. You will win where you are known and appreciated for who you really are. People recognize a fake performance immediately. In the moment you give people your hand and smile at them they know. Don´t pretend to be someone you aren´t.

If financial freedom is one of your values you will reach more in life by taking some well thought-out risks.

The eyes are the windows of the soul. In a millisecond people see in your eyes what´s going on in your heart, even before you say a word. You cannot be successful in selling until your pour your heart into it.

What touches you is obvious to others. With the vibration you communicate you win people over. Your authentic nature is always vibrating in unison with the right people.

During my travels around the world I was a guest at a weekly network meeting. During the introductions, each person had the opportunity to present themselves and their business. The gentleman before me was a doctor who owned his own practice. When it was my turn, I said: "I am not a doctor, but I too can heal." I stood up, pointed to my right breast-pocket and said: "Exactly here, where you usually find your wallet." Those present looked at me curiously. I explained that I specialized in guiding people to find their true calling, and in making this happen I have been able to build my business. The organizer of the meeting was aflame with excitement. She immediately organized a free evening event with me as the main speaker. More than 20 people came. Out of their excitement followed several other events, which brought me together with grateful clients. Several friendships emerged that exist to this day.

Learn the Art of Dialogue

Dialogue is a special art of communication with people that reveals their intelligence. A well-designed conversation brings out the brilliance and vitality in two or more people. The art of dialogue has been known since Socrates. Today only just a few salespeople take the time to learn it.

The modern advocate of the dialogue is David Boehm, an associate of Einstein. He was a physicist and philosopher. While many scientists are prone to giving speeches, he preferred to talk to people on the same level until their genius became visible. Dialogue doesn´t mean to interview someone or to ask the right questions. A dialogue is much more.

Have you ever spent time with a friend who really understood you? It was not important what you said. Everything was naturally perfect. Appreciation was present throughout the whole conversation. You felt connected and time flew by. The world stood still.

When I started learning these techniques, the feedback of my mentors wasn't always good. In order to acknowledge people on the same level, I had to let go of a lot of pride and arrogance. The moment I became amused by the opinions and moods of my fellows, I learned to express my appreciation. People around me started to take off their masks and show me the real person. Eventually, selling became more of a conversation between friends rather than an intellectual competition. Now, my relationships in business are light. They develop without effort.

In 2014 I spent the whole of November of my "Never-Ending Tour" in Montreal, Canada. I was looking for a massage parlor. At the front desk stood a nice young man that booked appointments. I asked him if he was the owner. He said: "Yes, I have two such businesses". I was curious and asked further: "How long have you been doing this?" He explained to me how he built this business with a partner, and described some challenges he had to overcome.
I noticed that he spoke with an accent and asked where he came from. "I come from Italy," he said, "and so I love food and women." We laughed. Now he was curious. I talked about my travels and my mission. Time stood absolutely still. We discovered that about 20 years ago we had attended the same training held by an international training company. Employees that came in asked if we were long-time friends. We met up later for lunch. Without having planned it, I won a new friend and client.

Surprise your Clients

The most interesting and inspiring events in your life are the unexpected ones. Something touches you when it is far beyond what you expect.

You can amuse people with actions or words. Authentic surprise pulls your clients out of their routine, allowing them to see themselves without a filter.

It is a great philosophy to give more than your clients expect.

To succeed in business, you need to do the right things at the right time. However, these plans are only part of a successful business. By adding the element of surprise, you create a special flair that catches the attention of the right people.

Success often comes serendipitously from unexpected events or happenings. You are often the surprise that your clients are looking for. When you stop trying to impress someone, your natural being will fascinate them. You show up in their lives as a person who will open a completely new world for them.

Allow yourself to live large. Don't try to control everything. Instead build a professional environment that is based on healthy chaos. Set up a framework where successful people can gather to generate interest in each other. Being able to embrace chaos multiplies your value to your clients.

Sales and marketing are forms of celebration. Start the party. Add the sense of celebration to your career. Create space to let delightful accidents happen by interacting with diverse people. Mix the visionaries who have fresh ideas with the managers who have their feet on the ground. The more colorful the group of people you work with, the more likely that unexpected things will happen.

I love coaching people, but my life isn't about pleasing everyone anymore. My second favorite activity is lying in the bathtub. So perhaps it was no coincidence that I was lying in the bathtub when a networking session with a potential customer took place. I considered whether I could allow this scenario to unfold. Then I decided to go ahead with it, because I would have found it totally in order if the situation were reversed. The appointment was set up for 12pm, but the customer appeared to be late. And so I began to shampoo my hair. A colleague was trying to reach me on Skype, so I took the call. Visibly surprised, the man on the screen looked at me with widened eyes.

"I am sorry, I thought we had an appointment," he said. "Am I interrupting you? Should I call back later?"

I laughed and replied: "No, everything is fine. I was waiting for you." Despite his initial surprise, we had an open, warm, and fruitful conversation. A day later I received a phone call from a client to whom the customer had recommended me as a coach.

He had told her about his experience. "At first I thought this person must be mad," he explained, "but through the course of our conversation it became clear to me that he is the right coach for me."

My first encounter in the bathtub created a lasting impression that led to interesting, lasting relationships with new clients.

Make your Clients' Goals your Own

Be sure to set goals that make business a delightful game, but then forget about your own goals. Play the game for the enjoyment of serving other people.

Imagine that you have somebody in your life who is committed to your success—someone who does everything necessary for your dreams to come true—someone who holds you accountable to your goals without any doubts as to your motivation or skills.

You can increase your influence by supporting your client. When you are focused on their goals you will develop a significant alliance.

It is impossible to resist someone who wholeheartedly agrees with your desires.

By making your clients' goals your own, you will reach a new level of partnership. Ask your clients what their goals are. Get a clear picture of what they want in their business and private lives. Let them know that their goals are important for you.

You are a member of your clients' team now. Be committed to the fulfillment of their desires. Their goals are your goals. Every time you help them take the next step your connection will grow deeper.

Team spirit is the connection of members on the same team. You are not able to play your game on your own. Help others win their game and you will win too. To ensure a long-lasting relationship with your clients, they need to know you are on their team. When you bond closely your clients, they will think first of you when they need something. With one deal you can succeed in the short term, but next week you face the same challenge to win new people for your business. Building lifelong partnerships is the secret of true success.

By rooting for your clients to get what they want, you become an essential part of their growing process. You service becomes more than a product or service. You become a reliable consultant in all aspects of their life. Naturally they will turn to you when they have a need that you can fulfill. In return they will start to look after you and help you to reach your goals.

In 1996, Halil Özgür from the firm "Özgür Fruits" was one of my best customers. Both of our businesses expanded. For Halil, this meant that his vegetable stand in the marketplace became too small. He allowed himself to take provisory measures, which was a pain-in-the neck for the market administration. At last he sent an application for an expansion, but was rejected by the authorities. He did not know what to do. Resigned, he told me about his seemingly hopeless situation and about how much he was counting on this expansion.

I declared that his project was also my goal. At first I asked myself: What may have been the reason for the declined application? In order to discover this, I went with Halil to the market-bureau. To our astonishment, the representative was exceptionally open and cooperative. The only condition from the side of the bureau was an orderly draft containing details of the project.

Two days later, I appeared at Halil's with an architect—a friend of mine. He prepared the necessary drawings, and the application was resubmitted. To Halil's great surprise, his proposal was accepted. He was very happy. Three months later, the planned expansion took place. This experience deepened our friendship. From this day onwards, Halil would give me valuable information about the price-politics of my competitors.

Build a Team

To have lasting success you need a team. Individuals generate limited outcomes. Only an organization can get consistent, powerful results.

Behind every superstar you will find a team that is doing the work to let the star shine. Before you can become a star, you have to learn to play as a team. The finest selling is a team play and the cooperation is the salt in the soup.

Internal competitions hinder trust. Team members who disable each other reduce the reliability of a company. People who can't count on each other become unreliable. In the past the main result of a campaign was often generated by the efforts of a single person. Heroes play an essential role in legends and myths.

In centuries past business was relatively simple. An intelligent person could learn everything they needed to know to operate a shop or sell a product. Today business is far more complicated. There are more products available and organizations are more complex.

Just as various sports require specialized people to play various positions, selling needs a team of specialists. Highly developed corporations employ overlapping patterns of communication. Salespeople tend to be clever and dynamic individuals who are used to thinking on their own. Bringing the best and most brilliant together in teams is a wonderful challenge.

Every single player has to spend time to learn the rules. You create the right environment by motivating them to build a sense of support.

People who serve each other create a spirit, which automatically serves the client. Teamwork requires a deep knowledge of human nature. Superficial social skills are not enough.

Fortunately you have everything you need for successful cooperation. Treat your clients and partners with respect. Just as you love and protect your family, you can extend that loving protection to your teammates.

Some people lose their innate sense of value in business. They let money make their decisions. Great salespeople are themselves under all conditions. They touch other people deeply with their integrity—their ability to integrate with associates and customers alike.

One of my biggest challenges I faced as a coach was at a gathering in Warsaw, Poland, in spring of 2010. A business-consultant whom I had befriended had the adventurous task of selling to 40 Polish self-employed farmers the necessity of creating a marketing cooperative. Through this collaboration they had a better chance of positioning themselves against the large supermarkets. For support, my friend brought me in as a keynote speaker.

The farmer in me knew that this situation required a very practical comprehensible method in order to reach these men. After my colleague held a 45 minute presentation with many slides, the resistance towards creating a union had become even stronger.

When I stepped in front of the room I told them about my own experiences as a cabbage farmer and my beginnings as a lone fighter. Then I distributed toothpicks among the participants. I invited them to break one in half. This was easy enough to do. Then I asked them to bundle 20 toothpicks and to try to break them. None of the farmers could break the bundle.

When I spoke I encountered resistance from those men, and even from the translator, however by sharing the power of togetherness experientially I was able to get this message across to the hardened lone operators:

"If from here on you continue to work alone, you will be catching nothing but small game. You will risk going hungry. Together, you will be able to hunt down a mammoth."

This experience produced an attraction that cut through the resistance and created curiosity about the power of teams.

Give Acknowledgements

People will believe you when the things you say are not in conflict with reality. Acknowledgement means to say something in a positive and direct way that describes how things really are.

People soon grow tired of being flattered. Superficial compliments create mistrust. There are clear ways to let people know that you appreciate their actions. Acknowledgement is a powerful pattern of communication that attracts people by speaking honestly what is actually happening. Acknowledgements bring you on the same page with others. Everyone can see what is actual. In the moment you acknowledge someone, you describe something they did or one of their qualities you appreciate. An acknowledgement shows a special quality the way it actually is. It is a simple honest mirror of an obvious truth shown in a positive way.

Criticism turns off the light in the eyes of people. Acknowledgment strengthens their vitality and self-confidence.

"I see you have new products" is an acknowledgement.

"I like your products" is a compliment.

"Your products are miserable" is a critique.

Acknowledgement provides a precise description of an event or a situation. When you give an acknowledgement you see your clients nodding and saying: "Yes, exactly."

Opinions are not very interesting. Irrefutable facts, spoken in a positive way, have a big influence on other people. No one can resist when you acknowledge a self-evident event.

Most successful salespeople use professional patterns of communication. Studies show that you get the best results by providing several acknowledgements before you ask for help or a recommendation. This method creates a bridge of attention. Your attention is on your client while his attention is on you. We are fascinated when someone is looking us in the eye and smiling at us.

We all want to get the best results possible. By acknowledging the actions of your clients you will have much to gain. If you invest time and effort to explore the best efforts of people you will lengthen the life of your business.

It is always easier to complain, blame and criticize others. You have to rehearse the art of acknowledgement. The investment of time and energy will be paid back with high return. A few minutes of honest interest and clear thinking can bring you thousands, even hundreds of thousands of dollars.

I remember a time around 20 years back when I entered the office of a client. At the time, I did not know the difference between a compliment and an acknowledgement. On the walls hung countless pictures with motifs and scenes from sailing. I said "You have absolutely beautiful pictures of sailing!"

My client turned to me and his face darkened visibly. "These damn pictures? I would prefer to throw them all out, but they belong to my father. And this office belongs to him as well. I look forward to having my own office." He was completely disgruntled.

With what I know now I would have acknowledged the nautical theme without any value judgment, or I would have focused on something he was actually doing. "You have a lot of pictures of sailing here. Do you sail?" That would have set up a condition to ask what he enjoyed and to follow his lead.

To me, this difference is gold. After I learned to acknowledge people, I was no longer in situations where I didn't know what to say, or where I accidentally cornered myself.

Remember Why You Sell

By relaxing and enjoying the moment you are like a breath of fresh air for your clients. When you are relaxed and calm you lift other people into a state of lightness. Your pleasure is the most important aspect of attraction in selling. Professional salespeople use their enthusiasm to raise the quality of life for those we serve.

If you are unable to amuse yourself your clients will think of you as just another boring person. They will feel your pressure and reflect it back to you. People spend much more time with you when it is fun to be around you.

The old way of selling refers to the clients' pain and offers solutions to problems. Of course it is helpful to free people from their problems, but most professionals can do that job. The new way of selling concentrates on lifting the human spirit by fulfilling the desires of other people.

As you develop the skills to discover the true desire of your clients, you will gain a strategic advantage. People feel that you see them in their true nature when you respond accurately to their inner needs.

It is established in human nature to seek pleasure and to avoid pain. Ask people what they want. Observe what theme will relax them. The thing that releases them from pressure is the key to winning their attention.

Busy people don't have much time today. They prefer to have quick meetings. But you can get your clients to stop the clock when you visit them. They will cancel appointments and give you their undivided attention. They will want to spend time with you because you bring them to the activities that bring them pleasure.

Most people feel stressed when you arrive to tell them about your product or service. When your meeting is about fulfilling their desires, you leave them relaxed and laughing. When your clients need something, they call you. They need something only you can offer, and often they call you to get recommendations for something you don´t specifically offer. When that happens, you have mastered the art of relationship selling.

By being interested in the needs of others, you become a source that they can rely on. Sometimes clients will send their friends to you just to share the connection.

In business you are always collecting a group of people with high integrity who naturally enjoy working together. Perhaps you meet for lunch, take walks, or exercise together. You talk and listen. You are building lifelong friendships by having fun together.

A lot of buyers meet salespeople all throughout the day. At the end of the day they have already heard everything. By being relaxed you stand out as special. When you emphasize enjoyment, selling will follow on its own. People remember you. They look forward to meeting you again. Meeting you inspires them. Your laughter lights up their day and builds a professional connection that endures for weeks or years.

Mornings were always peak-hours in hypermarkets. I was visiting my customer, Mr. Emir. We had not seen each other in a long time and I was curious how he and his business were doing. He had much to do, but asked me to take a seat in his office and we fell into conversation. Among other things, I asked him how many people he had in his service. Around 50, he answered. Then he told me the story of how 25 years ago, he started with nothing. He was the first Turkish wholesaler in all of Germany. This animated conversation continued and time flew by. Finally, his secretary came in the office to remind him of an appointment. He had spread himself thin between appointments. To my surprise, he asked his secretary to postpone the next appointment, and told her that he would not want to be further disturbed. So it was that a quick visitation turned into profound two-hour encounter, that we will never forget.

Be a Coach and Trainer

People love great coaches. They automatically resist salespeople. It is well worth your time to earn and use professional coaching strategies to be a source of inspiration for your clients.

A salesperson is focused on selling his product. Shift your attention off yourself and your desire to get a result. Discover the quality of your clients. As you start to develop their qualities you earn their respect.

A coach brings out the best in of you. Most people have had a great experience when a coach made a huge difference in their life. Perhaps it was a teacher, role model or a friend. As a coach you take total care of your clients. Increase your protecting nature by being kind. You are an empathetic person who honestly cares about others. Bring this quality into your selling.

The traditional way of selling is focused on reaching the goals of the sales organization. Coaching is concentrated on fulfilling the clients' goals. You go for the best in others. You fulfill their wishes. Instead of trying to sell them something, you wake up their desire to have it. Never force somebody to buy something, rather encourage their desire to buy what they want.

Who are your heroes? Many people have coaches that they recall fondly and with great respect. People admire coaches who inspire them. Almost everyone knows an inspiring coach or mentor. But there is hardly any salesperson who is known or loved. Along with selling your product or service, help your clients to develop their skills. Coaches don´t worry about profits. They are in the game of developing people.

The best salespeople help people develop themselves, therefore they stay connected to their clients.

As you believe in people and bring the best out in them you build a team of associates who will stand together in good times and in bad. Coaching builds lasting relationships.

I was visiting my friend Ali in a hypermarket in Berlin. We went in the canteen and talked about business. He revealed in conversation that he works seven days a week and sixteen hours a day and barely sees his family. His wife then came to him and asked, if he would go on a road-trip with her and their four children for Easter holidays. He could not see how he could possibly organize this. It appeared impossible to him. It was clear to me, that his invitation for me to visit entailed more than a sales call from his vegetable deliverer.

I asked him: "Ali, would it not be better if you somehow make it possible to spend a week away with your family?"

He answered: "Yes, of course I must do this, but what would happen to my company?"

I replied: "What would happen if tomorrow you break a leg and have to spend the day in the hospital? How would things proceed?"

He said: "Oh I have a few good colleagues, they would somehow manage. They can do it."

I noticed how he had opened up to the possibility of taking one week away from his company. The process was set in motion. He began to consider it.

For me, as a recently divorced man, the matter was relatively clear and so I said to him: "You have to do something for your family now. Otherwise at some point you will find yourself without one. And so that you see how much I like and respect you, I will tell you this, if you do not go on this trip with your family, I will not deliver to you anymore." He looked at me with widened eyes.

Three weeks later he called to tell me that he had actually gone on holiday. He thanked me from his heart and told me how good it had been for him, and also passed along warm greetings from his wife.

Learn How to Recognize Vitality

Most things we learn we are soon going to forget. In motivational training people become enthusiastic. This euphoria lasts for approximately a week. The same is true with what we study.

There is another way of learning that is deeper. There are some lessons you will never forget. The special skills you learn by practicing and getting feedback will continue to grow and expand over time. If you learn how to become aware of you effect on other people you will deepen your learning with every single action you take. Everytime you talk to people you will notice how their expressions change, whether they become brighter or darker. If you bring out their curiosity they will look and feel more alive. If you inundate them with information, their vitality will droop. Their eyes will glide deeper into their eye sockets.

By observing their eyes, body language, and changes in the texture and color of their skin, you can learn to distinguish when you are turning somebody on or off.

You see these physical transformations once you will become more sensitive to other people and to your effect on them. You will begin to develop strategies to help people get what they want. You start to develop your own unique selling method.

Customers don´t want to be dominated. Instead of pushing past their objection you can begin to notice how they want to help you. People want to buy. They want to be served. But they find their true happiness when they can serve you.

The moment you learn to see your impact on people, you will be shocked, at how often you bore people or push them away. Most sales training views the customer as an obstacle or opponent. You can learn to see past that adversarial paradigm.

In our early days we learned to get results by pushing someone else down. The education system trained all of us in win-lose and lose-lose principle. In business, as in sport, everyone finally loses.

Win-win is much more complex, but this strategy requires new skills. You have to learn by creating your own experiences. Develop profound communication skills. Take every seminar that helps you express yourself clearly and to know people better.

The basis of business is people. Your business will grow when your people skills grow. Great salespeople learn constantly. The most important skill to learn is how to inspire people.

During one of my first sales training, I made clear the distinction between "lights on and lights off" to the participants, and talked about the consequences of how people impact one another. In the end I asked them to do a role-play where they engaged in a selling conversation. To illustrate the process, we utilized candles. Those that played the clients held a candle in their hand to symbolize their mood. So long as the candle was lit, the customer was also "lit-up". The moment the seller turned off the light of the customer, the latter would blow out the candle. A very successful businessman, who considered himself a peak-performer in sales, was the first to take the role of the seller. A timid woman took the role of the customer. The seller began with a greeting: "Hello Sabine,....!" He did not go any further. The customer blew out the candle. The "seller" was completely shocked: "But I hadn't even begun." The customer looked at him and said almost self-consciously: "That might be, but you had already lost me."

Build your Business Network

A fisherman is more effective with a net than with a line. Similarly, you can earn more money when you change from individual selling to selling with your own sales network. Transform your customers and business relationships into a professional web that creates curiosity about you and your company.

A spider is weaving its web. Then the web multiplies the results. You can make the points on your own, or you can create a web that weaves together the efforts of many good people to assist you.

An individual can perform an adequate job in sales, but the connection between people creates an invisible magnet that produces far greater results.

If you give a man a fish he can eat for a day, but if you give him a fishing pole he can feed himself for many years. Show that same man how to build a sales web, and he will feed his family and contribute to his entire village.

When you need fast results it can seem counter-productive to focus on long lasting relationships. There is an art to split focus concentration—the act of providing a fish, a pole, and a net at the same time. To connect with people and communicate with them creates a network that will also boost your own career and make your life much lighter some day.

Networking is an excellent selling strategy to win a lot of people into your game. You don´t own the web. It is a structure that gives you the opportunity to provide for many people. A focused business web offers connections in which the customers can serve each other by offering complementary products and services. You can refer many professional services to someone else. That is how you build a web of interesting, interested people. Business is a system. Let the web do the heavy lifting for you.

The connection between people who are sharing their information is much stronger than the genius of one person. The common intelligence is brilliant. The information economy is complex. There are a lot of things to know and do. One person can't cover all the bases.

Imagine a scenario in which it is only you against the rest of the world. Now imagine there are hundreds of people who want to help you fulfill your desires. A wise person draws on the deep well of connections to earn a living by serving others.

Everyone isn't ready to play as a team. Other people can learn from you how to become honest and reliable. Your net becomes self-organizing as the reliable people find a certain place in it. That is the essence of a self-organized system. Team members learn from each other how to start and get tasks done on their own.

A business needs a strong leader. But a business web moves in concert without external commands. There is no authority figure who pushes lazy people to do something. Everyone is responsible for his or her learning and growth, otherwise they leave the team of their own volition.

A network of people who are selling and buying together create a strong force in business. We connect with honest people, many of whom will stay loyal, even though they change companies or build their own businesses.

When your friends climb up the ladder of success they will take you with them and introduce you to new markets. Your web might change participants, but the core will remain for your whole life.

My bookkeeper stepped in my office and asked if I had a minute for her. She told me about a friend of hers, the CEO of a major construction company, who was under great pressure and was facing significant challenges. "I have the feeling that you might be the right coach for him. In any case, he needs someone with experience in business, and who has been trained by highly respected coaches," she said. "I would really like to organize a meeting between the two of you."

I was really happy about the chance to talk with a successful man who was in crisis. I had found myself in transition between my two careers. During the day I would lead my vegetable wholesale company, and in the evenings and weekends, I would have time to cultivate my passion by offering sales and leadership training.

The meeting with the CEO did indeed take place. We found ourselves immediately on the same wavelength. In our first meeting we developed a plan tailored precisely to his firm. Subsequently I invited my mentor to this collaboration. He pledged his many years experience to service, and our collaboration led to a merging of our networks. Really good people came into contact that could never have been brought together through publicity or advertisement.

Tell Stories that Create Curiosity

In olden times people gathered around a campfire and told each other stories. Essentially they were sharing their lives and exchanging their experiences. Stories provide an essential way to make people feel what we feel and make them see what we see. Great storytellers awaken the imagination of people. They give life a deeper meaning. Everyone loves the storyteller.

Storytelling has an essential place in the sales process. Selling is based on three steps. First you have to create curiosity about your product or service. Then you have to invite people to buy. If they have hesitation or express objections you have to tell them your experiences with the product or service. You win their trust by telling them your own story.

Finally it is important to bring people back to your original theme by inviting them again to buy. When you combine storytelling with selling, people look forward to gathering around the fire of desire they feel when they meet with you.

```
    1                3
 Curiosity        Message

         2
      Invitation
```

The first step provides bait to attract buyers. The second step is the hook that brings them closer to a decision. That third step continues the story that makes you a legend in the minds of the people you serve. Creating curiosity by storytelling brings the customer to the turning point, where they can make a decision.

Storytelling is a craft. You use sentences as tools to describe your product very clearly, thus bringing people into the buying process.

Great storytellers capture rapt attention and lead people in the direction they want to go. An authentic salesperson describes true events in a way that raises your heartbeat.

Straight information has no magic in it to inspire the imagination. The spark that moves people has to arise from another person's imagination. You read it between the lines. If you tell the right story and use the right metaphor, they will fill the space in between with their own meaning. They feel that you speak to each of them in a very special way.

In storytelling you follow the same three steps as in selling. A story entertains and educates. If you want to inspire someone, don´t jump around and don´t wave your arms about wildly. Don´t tell people what they have to do. Don´t give them any advice. Tell a story. That way they bring their heart into the equation.

A good story doesn't need explanation or interpretation. We enjoy it together. It increases our common intelligence. When I explain something, I take the possibility away from my client to find his own meaning in the story. Storytelling uses the element of surprise to attract and entertain.

During an interview with a client named Hannes, I noticed his eyes suddenly light up as he was talking about how much he would love to buy an expensive sports car. He had the money, but he also had a lot of doubts. What would his co-workers say? And what about his neighbors? Most of all, how would his clients react to his new lifestyle? He wanted the car, but didn't quite trust himself to go for it. I told him the following story:

Many years ago, a father and son traveled to a city on the back of a donkey. The father rode on the donkey and the young boy walked alongside. A passerby complained to the father: "What kind of person are you, letting the young boy go on foot when you yourself are so powerfully built and still of good age!" Astonished and intimidated, the father and son switched places. From this point, the son sat on the donkey and the father led. They encountered another wanderer. This one yelled at the son on the donkey: "Shame on you, you miserable sprite! You who are young and strong, sit on the donkey and let your old father tread on foot." Father and son looked at each other astonished. To avoid criticism they both sat on the donkey. They continued their journey. It did not take long before they met another wanderer. He smirked: "What kind of people are you, torturing this donkey in this manner!" So what do you think happened next? The two carried the donkey to the city.

Six weeks later, I see Hannes drive proudly past me with his new black 911 Porsche Carrera convertible. By putting his values in perspective, he found new motivation and desire to grow his business.

Be Flexible in Changing Times

We are used to assuming that we know what´s going on. This mistake costs us a lot of business because we unconsciously believe we know what other people want and need. A lot of businesses fall by the wayside because they miss a chance to react to changing desires. Few salespeople take adequate time to explore what people really want.

Curious people attach importance to subtle distinctions in the eyes and faces of other people. Have the needs of my clients changed in the last month, or even in the last minute? Be careful with the concepts in your mind. Your experiences are worthy, but they aren't always in tune with reality. Your memories don´t tell you what is in front of your eyes. Attention and humility are helpful to clear your perceptions so that you can notice changes in the people you serve.

On a stormy night on a bad road the most experienced driver drives slowly. By being aware of the danger the most courageous person will become humble and awake. It is not so easy to pay attention to our clients at every moment. We make assumptions and ignore warning signs. The danger of losing them is hard to see. Force yourself every moment to see what is the same and what is different. In business the fittest will survive. That means you have to be more flexible than the others. Things change quickly. Your advantage is to see changes first.

Have you ever walked through a forest? Have you ever walked through a tree? To see the difference between the forest and the trees is very important.

Pattern recognition is a method of observation that will give you distinctions others don´t have. You learn pattern recognition by working and playing with highly advanced teachers, coaches, and mentors. Noticing patterns of behavior and communication give you more accurate indications of changing needs in the people who make up your market.

Notice how you read this book. What is the difference between what you already know and this information? People with a restricted view tend to think they already know what they hear or see. Curious people allow information to touch them in new ways.

The mind sees things in chunks. One thing often seems like the other, but slightly different. Clever people recognize how special every single event and person is. When you are able to see differences you can adjust your perceptions and change your strategies and tactics.

Business is a complex game with ever-changing rules. Words can't sort out the subtle differences in how the game is played.

Lots of words sound similar—listening, values, benefit—but their meanings change. To adjust yourself, you have to hear what´s not spoken. Adjustment means to adapt your approach in reaction to your clients' needs.

There is a paradox here. The more you adjust yourself to fit with other people, the more you will find your true self. So the art of being yourself is the craft of becoming who you need to be in the lives of others.

I spent a weekend in Amsterdam, Netherlands. I was wandering down the streets and walked past a fast-food restaurant. Here I saw four young women wearing headscarves, sitting down eating hamburgers. I paused. Before my mind's eye I saw my vegetable vendor business going down the drain. My business idea was based on the exclusive delivery to wholesalers of traditional Turkish vegetables. I became hot then cold. If Turkish people here are consuming American food, then even in Germany traditional food might not have great prospects. Such a cultural shift could be fatal to my business. How should I think about this erroneous belief that my business strategy would succeed, even while people around me were changing their eating habits. I had enjoyed great success in the previous 12 years with my business model. Now I needed to come up with something new.

I made a decision. I would not force my products to fit the trends, instead, I would use the know-how built over two generations on raising cabbage to create completely new markets. Two years later I delivered a specially developed brand, which I named Jaroma Cabbage, to four of out the five largest supermarket chains in Germany. For this brand we received innovation prizes from the Chamber of Commerce and the Financial Times of Germany.

Train Like an Athlete

Did you ever wonder why some salespeople achieve vastly greater results than others?

In every sales team there are a few superstars who earn twice as much as the others. A select few earn up to 10 times more than the others. Why is this happening? Do they have more talent? Or are their other factors at play? Is it possible for you to become a top performer in your field?

The simple truth is there are no "born" salespeople. I have observed excellent results from extroverted people, and also witnessed outstanding results from introverted ones. There are great salespeople with low and high intelligence quotients. Great results are often achieved by highly talented, and at the same time from less talented people. Many winners are especially attractive—others less so. Sometimes you will see similar outcomes from bold, active people and from quiet, calm people.

In the end there is only one criterion that separates winners from the losers in the game of business. The former train constantly. Let me remind you that in selling skill is the central factor when it comes to earning success.

Airbus has taken over more and more market share from Boeing because of one reason—the great success in sales from the European management. Continuous improvement is the secret recipe of excellent salespeople. Great experts in the business world reach the top because of the ability to sell better than the others. Leaders like Elon Musk are able to sell their products, their company and their vision. They win other people over to their game. They might have special technical ability, but they had to learn selling, just like you and me. They mastered their skill through constant improvement.

The best salesman I ever met was a simple man. His behavior was humble and disarming. I noticed how I was giving him advice in selling.

Suddenly I discovered that he was one of the top leaders in the country. "Why did you allow me to give you tips in selling," I asked him, "when you obviously know more than me?"

"I never met somebody from whom I couldn't learn something." he said. This was the day I opened a new level of respect for the learning process.

I know somebody who sells business machines. He never took a training unless it was sponsored from his distributors. His salespeople shared the same bias about advanced training. Not surprisingly, his company lost money every year. Every time I recommended a sales training to him, he offered the same excuses. He had no time or no money.

You might hear this excuse in your own career. Over the long run such a limited perspective continues to shrivel.

Olympic athletes are always in training. They aren't looking for more time to watch TV or spend time with their friends. They are always kicking a ball or doing push-ups. Training is the background for everything they do. If you want to work hard for small results, then avoid training. But if you want to play hard with outstanding results than you have to train continuously, just as you would to prepare for victory in the Olympic games.

One day I met with a long-standing client to discuss strategy. He was facing one of the most challenging phases of his life as a businessman. The following day he had a decisive meeting with a large customer. The results of the meeting would determine whether his firm with 70 employees would survive. Over the years he had invested in regular seminars of sales and leadership training for himself and his employees. For his efforts he was often criticized by those around him. He was often met with hostility about how much money he was spending on seemingly unproductive activities. Now his foresight would pay off.
During our talk, we discussed the situation and crafted a plan. The next day he sat well-armed at the negotiations. The committee was composed of six people. With great alertness he observed them. His lightness, his appreciative feedback, and the manner in which he yielded at the right moment, enabled him to win over his customers and come to a lucrative large contract. The years of regular training paid off massively on a single day, and brought him much needed success at the right time.

Make Sales your Priority

Imagine a prehistoric hunter who prefers to stay at home with his family instead of going hunting. As long as they have enough to eat he would have the luxury of playing with his children and giving unlimited attention to his wife. But when food ran short, conditions would change. He would become a liability and his family would become a burden to the community. They would be met with disapproval. Eventually his wife would have to leave him. He would lose the most important thing in his life.

Selling is a craft. Sometimes it rises up to an art, but much of the time it is hard work. Selling requires commitment and passion.

The rules of business are the same for everyone. Anyone can learn to sell in an effective way. But professional dedication is the highest priority. Without constant, consistent effort you won't gain the skills you need to bring home the bacon.

Good selling is based on character and technique. Your psychological state is the tools of this craft. The moment you decide to have career as a salesperson you have to make another decision. Do you want to have a good income or do you want to suffer with every single bill you get?

High performance players in all fields make business their priority. Ironically, all arenas in your life become better when you put your craft in the primary position. The reason people fail to provide and protect their loved ones is often due to a lack of money. Scarcity disturbs businesses, families, and personal friendships. You can't buy happiness or loyalty with money, but a good cash flow creates an environment where these qualities can grow.

You need as much time for an excellent career as for an average one. There is a time to live and a time to die. There is a time to work and a time to rest. When you pay your selling the time and attention it requires, the benefits will flow into every aspect of your life. Materialism is not immoral. It doesn't disturb nature. It is the opposite. If you offer a product you believe in, you will change the conditions necessary to make the world a better place.

In the game of business, one is producing, one is transporting, one is selling, one is buying, and one is consuming. Selling is an invisible web of useful, interactive connections that nurtures families and communities. Prosperity provides the opportunity to build better and cleaner products and to improve the production itself.

Whatever your values are, put them together to put selling in the first position. This perspective will support your other values. Effective selling brings you the material goods that enable you to make a contribution to the people you love. The financial freedom to travel and purchase essential good makes your life worthwhile, full and valuable.

I recall very clearly how in 1989 I stood at the very beginning of building my vegetable business. Most of the time I was still working as a farmer, active in vegetable production. I was a part-time seller in my own small business when I took my very first steps into the larger field of sales and distribution.

It was a great challenge for me to begin calling customers directly. I would have preferred a thousand times over to be stooping over a cold field in the rain and working the land, rather than sitting in a dry office calling customers. But I knew that if I did not act unwaveringly in this new realm, the future which I had envisioned would not come to be realized.

My father was a farmer before me. He had a different opinion about my future. I was forced to defend myself constantly for the time I devoted to selling. So I carved out time to face my fear of being rejected by customers. Over the phone I hung a saying: "Winners never quit and quitters never win." And so I picked up the phone and began calling customers in the hypermarkets. I am convinced that adapting my business model to include professional selling was the beginning of my success. Because I also invested time to learn the skills of professional selling, I eventually was able to grow my business far beyond my expectations.

Expand your Horizons

Salespeople are often specialists. Some excel at selling material products. Others have the knack for selling intangible ones, like services or ideas. If you are better at selling training than at selling cars, you would benefit by taking time to learn how to sell material things. If it is easier for you to sell products, you can expand your skills by learning to sell ideas.

When Michael Jordan realized that he was less effective dribbling with the left hand, he concentrated on training during the off-season. People have two eyes, two legs and two arms. Even our brain has a left and a right side. By developing the other side you activate strong learning strategies.

Some people work well on teams, while others prefer to work alone. When you learn to respect other points of views you will have a lot more people driving your success. Someone who sells machines might not see the value in self-help groups or personal coaching. But if you take time to explore a new field that is not so easy to understand, you will also increase your skill of connecting with a greater variety of people in your preferred arena.

One of my friends refused to take trainings in soft skills because in his opinion it was enough to know his product. When I finally won him to participate in a training he got an unexpected triple benefit out of it.

On one hand he improved his sales skills. On the other hand he discovered a new network of buyers for his products. After all, teachers use products too, and they tend to make referrals to a large number of people. Lastly, his private life became better when he used his new people skills to connect deeper with other people.

Don´t be concerned about your weaknesses. Concentrate on the things you are good at. But don´t ignore the fields in which you can improve. Expand your horizons and explore new fields whenever possible. Open the part of you that is not so curious about new things. The reward is worth the risk.

Create open questions. Allow other people to train you. People love to talk. They soon grow tired of listening. The favorite theme of people is to talk about themselves. They want to share their hopes and fears. They want to let everyone know about their families, talents, and heroic deeds. The person that will let them talk will become the receiver for their attention. Questions are tools to open hearts and minds. A good salesperson carries around a well-prepared toolbox filled with questions that win the respect of others.

What do you love to do? What is important for you? Tell me about your company. Such open questions give people a chance to speak from the heart.

Closed questions have yes or no as an answer. Sometimes a closed question can be useful for bringing someone to a decision, but with open questions, people can express themselves fully.

People develop themes you would have never imagined. They will talk to you in a special manner so that you can see how you can sell to them.

My self-conception is that of a shy man, who is reluctant to approach strangers. In order to overcome this fear, I challenged myself. In April of 2013 I started my Never-Ending Tour. This meant that I would go alone to new cities throughout the world where I knew no one, in order to meet new people and develop friendships with strangers. The challenge was to hold talks in each city and to serve people in the building of their business. My great adventure required the act of speaking to people with the aim of sharing myself with them. By offering help and asking for it when necessary, I confronted my biggest fear. The tour led me through the US, Canada, China, Europe, New Zealand and Australia. Eventually I plan to reach every corner of the world. Not only am I getting to know many wonderful people, but somewhere along the way I forgot about my anxiety and also the fact that my English speaking capacities weren't very strong.

To this day, I enjoy releasing myself into unknown situations. There, the possibility of encountering something unexpected is higher. Slowly but surely I parted from my old self-conception. In my travels I discovered that reality is quite different from the image we have created of it.

About the Authors

Dylan Watts

Dylan Watts is a full-blood entrepreneur and adventurer. His passion: empowering people and enabling them to grow.

As a professional trainer, business coach and mentor, he supports innovative people and organizations.

Through his background in nature and farming he has developed a particular awareness of healthy development processes that lead to lasting success. Dylan breaks apart old structures and weaves the individual pieces into a harmonious and collaborative whole.

As a people-grower, his goal is to bring people's hidden talents and capacities to light. Aside from creativity and enthusiasm, he brings out the inner brilliance in every individual.

He doesn't just develop them into outstanding business-people, but rather leads them on a path where they can fulfill their unique desires and dreams.

Dylan is particularly drawn to the subjects of sales and leadership. On these matters he can draw from many years of experience in his own business.

In the late 80s, as the farming industry began to decline, he started a new enterprise as a street vendor. His eagerness and his strong conviction showed that everyone can achieve anything if they truly want it.

Sometime later Dylan was delivering vegetables to Turkish wholesalers across Germany. He sums up his business philosophy in one sentence: "Your children will continue to do business with my children". As his business grew he reached the top of his field, delivering vegetables for the "Big Five". His example shows that anyone can learn to sell.

Today Dylan Watts is an expert in the realm of people skills. He enjoys sharing his wide-reaching experience to help those interested in developing themselves.

Dr. Gerhard Dollansky

If you have ever used easy and intuitive software, then you understand what Gerhard Dollansky does. He specializes in rendering complicated applications simple enough to be intuitively understood and easily utilized. Through this he made a name for himself in IT. His user-friendly designed technology is used today across wholesale businesses and industrial customers. "User-friendly" is his overarching theme.

He relies on this talent also in his work as an advisor. He employs the tools described in this book, whereby complex work processes are simplified and made easy to master. Through these tools, extraordinary results in quality and quantity can be achieved.

Gerhard recognizes effective processes and can communicate them with fine sensitivity. The usual sales tricks have always repelled him. It was important to him to find a way to win clients without resorting to manipulation. He has devoted a significant amount of time to the study of soft-skills. From this emerged *Forget about Selling*, which presents the theme of selling through attraction.

Gerhard Dollansky shares his knowledge as a Keynote Speaker on conferences. He leads workshops and master-mind groups, and his clients value him as a competent advisor and mentor.

Gerhard Dollansky has a PhD in Economics. His passions include Korean martial art Taekwon-Do. He is a marathon runner, a family man, and t father of two children. Currently he lives in Munich, Germany.

We would love to hear from you!

By reading this book we know that you are on the right path of growing your people skills and your team. If you are curious how to improve your team or sales people, here are the next steps.

Contact us for a free 30 minute coaching session.

Find out about our webinars:
Forget About Selling online.

Sign up for the monthly newsletter on the website www.dylanwatts.tv and check the calendar for events in your city.

The authors would love to hear what you think about this book! If you have a raving review about how it helped you build your business and customer relationships, or any comments or suggestions about the content of this book, please take time to write them down and send them to:

Jaro – Peoplegrowers GmbH
Dylan Watts & Gerhard Dollansky
Theater Platz 3
52062 Aachen
Germany
www.forget-about-selling.com
office@DylanWatts.tv
+1 512 893-0637 (Dylan)
+1 512 545-2227 (Gerhard)

List of available trainings and speeches from the authors:

- Coaching For Leaders
- Forget About Selling
- The Innovation In You

Please check the website
www.forget-about-selling.com

www.ingramcontent.com/pod-product-compliance
Lightning Source LLC
Chambersburg PA
CBHW060407190526
45169CB00002B/786